MASSIVE

Journey of the ELEPHANT SEALS

BY ANNERENEÈ GOYETTE

Gareth Stevens
PUBLISHING

Please visit our website, www.garethstevens.com. For a free color catalog of all our high-quality books, call toll free 1-800-542-2595 or fax 1-877-542-2596.

Cataloging-in-Publication Data

Names: Goyette, AnneReneé.
Title: Journey of the elephant seals / AnneReneé Goyette.
Description: New York : Gareth Stevens Publishing, 2019. | Series: Massive animal migrations | Includes index.
Identifiers: ISBN 9781538216460 (pbk.) | ISBN 9781538216453 (library bound) | ISBN 9781538216477 (6 pack)
Subjects: LCSH: Elephant seals--Juvenile literature.
Classification: LCC QL737.P64 G69 2019 | DDC 599.79'4--dc23

First Edition

Published in 2019 by
Gareth Stevens Publishing
111 East 14th Street, Suite 349
New York, NY 10003

Copyright © 2019 Gareth Stevens Publishing

Designer: Katelyn E. Reynolds
Editor: Joan Stoltman

Photo credits: Cover, p. 1 Kevin Schafer/Corbis Documentary/Getty Images; cover, pp. 1–24 (background) Vadim Georgiev/Shutterstock.com; cover, pp. 1–24 (background) CS Stock/Shutterstock.com; p. 5 © iStockphoto.com/ bill_lloyd; p. 7 Timothy Riese/Shutterstock.com; p. 9 Dennis W Donohue/Shutterstock.com; p. 11 Richard Herrmann/Minden Pictures/Getty Images; p. 13 Paul Souders/Corbis Documentary/Getty Images; p. 15 David Osborn/Shutterstock.com; p. 17 (map) Serban Bogdan/Shutterstock.com; p. 17 (inset) Bildagentur Zoonar/ Shutterstock.com; p. 19 CodeOne/Wikipedia.org; p. 21 JeremyRichards/Shutterstock.com.

Printed in the United States of America

CPSIA compliance information: Batch #CS18GS: For further information contact Gareth Stevens, New York, New York at 1-800-542-2595.

CONTENTS

WORDS IN THE GLOSSARY APPEAR IN **BOLD** TYPE
THE FIRST TIME THEY ARE USED IN THE TEXT.

The Amazing ELEPHANT SEAL!

Elephant seals are ocean mammals, like whales and dolphins. Although they all have hair, breathe air, and feed milk to their young, elephant seals are quite different from other ocean mammals. Elephant seals rest, **molt**, give birth, nurse, and **mate** on land!

There are two species, or kinds, of elephant seals. The northern species lives in the Pacific Ocean from Mexico to Alaska. They come on land in Mexico and California. The southern species lives on land and in waters south of the **equator.**

⟩ THERE'S MORE! ⟨

THE LONG NOSES ON MALES LOOK A LOT LIKE ELEPHANT TRUNKS! THEY CAN GROW TO BE 2 FEET (0.6 M) LONG. WHEN FILLED WITH AIR, THESE NOSES MAKE CALLS THAT CAN BE HEARD MILES AWAY!

Male northern elephant seals can weigh up to 5,000 pounds (2,300 kg)—that's twice as much as their females! Male southern elephant seals can weigh almost 9,000 pounds (4,100 kg)—that's 4 times heavier than their females!

male

female

On LAND

Elephant seals have a double **migration**, which means they migrate to land twice a year. They're the only animals in the world known to do that, though scientists may discover more in the future!

Because they only eat underwater food, elephant seals don't eat when they're on land. They also don't poop, pee, drink water, or even breathe much on land! This is all done to save **energy.** It also makes molting, birthing, nursing, and mating happen faster so they can get back to eating!

THERE'S MORE!

ELEPHANT SEALS SPEND AROUND 3 MONTHS OF EACH YEAR ON LAND. THAT MUCH TIME SPENT WITHOUT FOOD MEANS THEY CAN LOSE ABOUT 35 PERCENT OF THEIR WEIGHT!

An area on land where elephant seals stay is called a rookery. A group of elephant seals is called a colony. The group of females around the top male, called the alpha male, is known as his harem.

That's One BIG PUP!

One of elephant seals' two migrations is for birthing, nursing, and mating. Females give birth at night within a week of arriving on land. They nurse their babies, called pups, for 23 days with some of the richest milk in the world. During that time, pups grow 3 to 4 times larger because of that milk!

After nursing, females and males mate. Then the adults head into the ocean to eat. Pups stay a few months teaching themselves how to swim and living off the weight from their mother's rich milk.

> ### THERE'S MORE!
>
> ELEPHANT SEAL PUPS CAN'T ENTER THE WATER IMMEDIATELY. FIRST, THEY MOLT 10 TO 34 DAYS AFTER THEY'RE BORN. NOW THEY CAN SPEND NIGHTS IN THE WATER, PRACTICING SWIMMING, DIVING, AND FINDING FOOD IN THE DARK.

Swimming MANY MILES

Once they're back in the ocean, elephant seals swim 15,000 to 20,000 miles (24,000 to 32,000 km) alone each year as they dive for food. They need fatty food—and lots of it!—to gain back the weight they lost on land!

Elephant seals spend almost 80 percent of their life in cold, deep ocean waters. Blood is pushed away from their skin to keep their insides warm. But the skin dies without blood. They head to land and molt for 3 to 5 weeks to grow new skin!

THERE'S MORE!

SCIENTISTS AREN'T SURE HOW ELEPHANT SEALS KNOW THE WAY FROM THEIR BIRTHING AND MOLTING LAND TO THEIR FEEDING AREAS. THEY MAY USE THE STARS, SOUNDS, OR EVEN HAVE SPECIAL PARTS IN THEIR BODIES THAT WORK LIKE A **COMPASS!**

- - - > Elephant seals' blood flows in a special way to keep them warm. **Arteries** carrying warm blood from the heart share their heat with nearby veins carrying cold blood to the heart!

SUPERDIVERS

In the ocean, elephant seals dive day and night. At the beginning of each dive, their tail fins push water. The rest of the dive is **gliding** down deeper and deeper! Scientists once saw a female elephant seal dive over a mile (1.6 km)!

Elephant seals can stay underwater for 2 hours. They even sleep on some dives! They do this by slowing down their heartbeat and breathing and by moving blood only to the heart and brain. They also do this on land to save energy!

> **THERE'S MORE!**
>
> ELEPHANT SEALS ARE CARNIVORES, WHICH MEANS THEY EAT MEAT. FEMALES MOSTLY EAT SQUID. MALES EAT SMALL SHARKS, RAYS, AND FISH THAT SWIM ALONG THE OCEAN FLOOR.

It's dark underwater, so elephant seals have special eyes that can see 10 times more light than ours! They dive deeper during the day—not because of the dark, but because that's when yummy animals are out!

13

Northern ELEPHANT SEALS

Northern elephant seals have the longest migration of any mammal on Earth. They travel 12,400 miles (20,000 km) a year. Scientists aren't sure why they chose Californian and Mexican beaches to migrate to—there are many beaches closer to their ocean feeding areas!

Northern elephant seal males arrive on land in late November to fight each other for mating rights. Only the males who win the fights get to mate, and sometimes the fights can be bloody! Females arrive a few weeks later to birth and nurse.

> ### THERE'S MORE!
>
> FEMALES RETURN IN APRIL TO MOLT. MALES DON'T RETURN TO MOLT UNTIL JULY. PART OF THE TIMING DIFFERENCE IS BECAUSE THE MORE **PREGNANT** A FEMALE IS, THE MORE ENERGY SHE NEEDS TO MIGRATE. AN EARLIER MOLT SAVES ENERGY!

Males vs. FEMALES

Female northern elephant seals swim to different parts of the ocean than males of the species. Females head north and west to eat in the open ocean. Males travel to a much more dangerous part of the ocean because the food there is better.

As long as an orca whale doesn't eat them, male northern elephant seals can find enough crabs, clams, lobsters, and other ocean floor animals to gain all the weight they need for fighting and traveling!

THERE'S MORE!

FEMALE NORTHERN ELEPHANT SEALS SPEND ABOUT 300 DAYS A YEAR AT SEA. THAT'S ABOUT 50 DAYS MORE THAN MALES. THEY EAT ANIMALS THAT LIVE BETWEEN THE SHORE AND OCEAN FLOOR, ESPECIALLY SQUID!

Males swim 1,000 to 2,000 miles (1,000)
farther than females as they curve around landforms
underwater. Females don't have that kind of time—they
need to find food and eat!

NORTHERN ELEPHANT SEAL MIGRATION

ALASKA

CANADA

male migration

UNITED STATES

female migration

Pacific Ocean

17

ELEPHANT SEALS

Southern elephant seals are the largest seals on Earth! There's also no other mammal whose females and males are so different!

The water they live in is very cold, but rich in fish and squid. When it's time to move to land, they're just as likely to choose an icy or snowy coast as they are to choose a rocky beach! Whether it's for molting or giving birth and mating, southern elephant seals migrate up to 1,240 miles (2,000 km) each time they need to be on land.

THERE'S MORE!

FEMALE SOUTHERN ELEPHANT SEALS HAVE AROUND 7 PUPS IN THEIR LIFETIME, ONE AT A TIME. THEY'RE PREGNANT FOR HALF THEIR LIFE!

Though southern elephant seals mainly live in the cold oceans and on the islands near the South Pole, a few have been found near the equator! Southern elephant seals have also been born in Australia, New Zealand, and South Africa.

SOUTHERN ELEPHANT SEAL RANGE

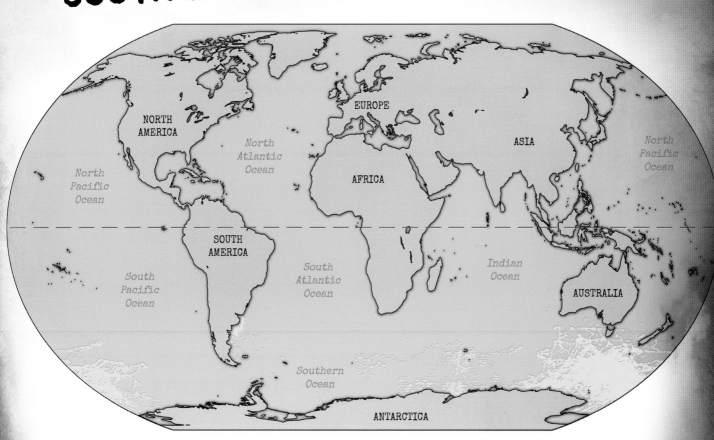

southern elephant seals

Elephant Seals
IN DANGER!

Not long ago, elephant seals almost died out. In the 18th and 19th centuries, both northern and southern species were hunted for their **blubber.** Thankfully, there are now laws against hunting them. Though there once were as few as 20, there are now close to 225,000 northern elephant seals! Southern elephant seals are doing even better with at least 600,000!

Elephant seals are a very important part of the ocean food web. Let's keep them—and the beaches they return to year after year—safe!

> ## THERE'S MORE!
>
> WHEN A WINTER STORM OFF THE COAST OF CALIFORNIA OR MEXICO HAS LOTS OF RAIN, IT'S OFTEN DEADLY FOR NORTHERN ELEPHANT SEAL PUPS. NOT YET ABLE TO SWIM, 80 PERCENT OF NEW PUPS HAVE BEEN KNOWN TO WASH AWAY INTO THE SEA DURING STORMS.

A word of advice if you should see an elephant seal:
If the seals are looking at you, you're too close! Stay at least
100 feet (30 m) away, so that they don't feel scared.

GLOSSARY

artery: one of the tubes that carry blood from the heart to all parts of the body

blubber: a thick layer of fatty matter under the skin that keeps an animal's insides warm in the cold

compass: a tool for finding directions by using a magnetic needle

energy: power used to do work

equator: an imaginary circle around the middle of Earth that is the same distance from the North Pole and the South Pole

glide: to move in a smooth and graceful way

mate: to come together to make babies

migration: the act of moving from one area to another for feeding or having babies

molt: to shed old fur and skin while new fur and skin grows in

pregnant: carrying an unborn baby in the body

FOR MORE INFORMATION

Books

Furstinger, Nancy. *12 Marine Animals Back From the Brink*. North Mankato, MN: 12-Story Library, 2015.

Holing, Dwight. *Incredible Journeys: Amazing Animal Migrations*. New York, NY: Kingfisher, 2011.

Owings, Lisa. *Elephant Seal*. Minneapolis, MN: Bellwether Media, 2014.

Websites

Northern Elephant Seals
gtopp.org/about-gtopp/animals/northern-elephant-seals.html
This page has a map that shows you exactly where the elephant seals this group studies are *right now*!

View the Seals
elephantseal.org/view.htm
Watch this live video feed of the elephant seal habitat in California—with sound!

Zoomable Panorama: Elephant Seals
animals.nationalgeographic.com/animals/gigapan/elephant-seals/
Imagine you're surrounded by elephant seals with this awesome photograph!

INDEX